Returning Home

RESETTLEMENT AND REINTEGRATION OF DETAINEES
RELEASED FROM THE U.S. NAVAL BASE IN GUANTÁNAMO BAY, CUBA

March 2009

International Human Rights Law Clinic
University of California, Berkeley, School of Law

Human Rights Center
University of California, Berkeley

INTERNATIONAL HUMAN RIGHTS LAW CLINIC, UNIVERSITY OF CALIFORNIA, BERKELEY, SCHOOL OF LAW

The International Human Rights Law Clinic (IHRLC) designs and implements innovative human rights projects to advance the struggle for justice on behalf of individuals and marginalized communities through advocacy, research, and policy development. The IHRLC employs an interdisciplinary model that leverages the intellectual capital of the university to provide innovative solutions to emerging human rights issues. The IHRLC develops collaborative partnerships with researchers, scholars, and human rights activists worldwide. Students are integral to all phases of the IHRLC's work and acquire unparalleled experience generating knowledge and employing strategies to address the most urgent human rights issues of our day. For more information, please visit www.humanrightsclinic.org.

HUMAN RIGHTS CENTER, UNIVERSITY OF CALIFORNIA, BERKELEY

The Human Rights Center promotes human rights and international justice worldwide and trains the next generation of human rights researchers and advocates. We believe that sustainable peace and development can be achieved only through efforts to prevent human rights abuses and hold those responsible for such crimes accountable. We use empirical research methods to investigate and expose serious violations of human rights and international humanitarian law. In our studies and reports, we recommend specific policy measures that should be taken by governments and international organizations to protect vulnerable populations in times of war and political and social upheaval. For more information, please visit hrc.berkeley.edu.

Contents

EXECUTIVE SUMMARY

On January 22, 2009, President Obama signed an executive order to close the detention facilities in Guantánamo Bay Naval Base within 12 months. A comprehensive plan for closing the camp should include a resettlement and reintegration program for detainees released from the facility since 2002. Our data indicate that social stigma, unemployment, and impairments to mental and physical health hinder efforts of former detainees to re-establish their lives after release from custody.

United States support for reintegration efforts is strategically and morally justified. Such efforts will (1) protect U.S. national security, (2) help repair the U.S. image abroad, (3) enable former detainees to lead productive lives, and (4) strengthen multilateral cooperation to combat terrorism worldwide.

WE PROPOSE THAT THE UNITED STATES:

» *Design a resettlement and reintegration policy to minimize the social stigma experienced by former Guantánamo detainees.* A case-by-case process should be implemented to enable former detainees to clear their names and encourage community members to assist released detainees as they reintegrate into their communities.

» *Provide released detainees with immediate short-term financial assistance and support for sustainable livelihoods.* A comprehensive reintegration program should provide immediate assistance, as well as support detainees to secure sustainable employment and income for the long-term. Preparation for reentry into the job market should begin before release. Job training and job-creation programs, such as small- and medium-scale enterprise development initiatives, should also be a key part of the program and target local labor markets. Such support should afford released detainees an opportunity to craft their own solutions to overcome the economic challenges they face, and give them a sense of autonomy and ownership in their reintegration.

» *Support the provision of mental and physical health services for released detainees who seek such assistance.* These services should be offered in conjunction with other reintegration services, such as job training and family support. This integrated approach should address the relationship of economic hardships and mental health problems.

» *Ensure that reintegration programs are developed and implemented in partnership with local communities.* Local religious and civic organizations should be involved in the design and implementation of reintegration programs to secure the legitimacy of reintegration efforts in the home countries of former detainees. The U.S. government should develop a comprehensive resettlement and reintegration policy overseen by a high-level State Department official. However, it may be appropriate for the United States to support in-country implementation through local independent nongovernmental organizations, with appropriate monitoring and oversight.

Introduction

On January 22, 2009, President Barack Obama signed an executive order to close the detention facilities in Guantánamo Bay within 12 months.[1] The order requires an immediate review of the 245 detainees still held in Guantánamo to determine whether they should be prosecuted, transferred, or released.[2] Upon issuing the order, President Obama said: "The message that we are sending the world is that the United States intends to prosecute the ongoing struggle against violence and terrorism and we are going to do so vigilantly and we are going to do so effectively and we are going to do so in a manner that is consistent with our values and our ideals."[3]

Closing Guantánamo is necessary to repair the U.S. image at home and abroad. But closure is only a first step toward that goal. Any comprehensive plan for closing the facility should also include a resettlement and reintegration program for released detainees either in their country of origin, the United States, or a third country. This paper outlines the elements of such a program and its rationale.

To date, more than 525 of the approximately 770 known detainees who have been held at Guantánamo since 2002—over 65% of the total population—have been released.[4] The closure of Guantánamo will only increase this number. Available data suggest that few released detainees have received reintegration assistance from the United States, home governments, or private organizations.[5]

The United States should play an active role in reintegration efforts. Support for such programs will (1) protect U.S. national security, (2) help repair the U.S. image abroad, (3) enable former detainees to lead productive lives, and (4) strengthen multilateral cooperation in the effort to combat terrorism worldwide. "To truly achieve victory," writes Secretary of Defense Robert Gates, "the United States needs a military whose ability to kick down the door is matched by its ability to clean up the mess and even rebuild the house afterward."[6] A U.S.-supported resettlement and reintegration program for former detainees is a crucial step in "rebuilding the house."

United States leadership on this issue is consistent with—if not compelled by—this nation's commitment to principles of fairness and humanitarianism. The available data indicate that the battlefield screening process used in Afghanistan to identify members of the Taliban or Al Qaeda was flawed from the start.

As a result, many of the men transferred to Guantánamo were taken in error or never posed a serious threat to U.S. security. According to a Seton Hall report based entirely upon U.S. government documents, only 4 percent of the detainees held in Guantánamo were fighting at the time of their apprehension; moreover, only 5 percent of detainees at the camp were apprehended directly by the United States.[7] The rest were captured by non-U.S. forces, including Pakistani and Afghan tribal militias and bounty hunters, in exchange for cash rewards paid by the United States.[8] Contrary to longstanding law enforcement, intelligence, and previous military practice,[9] the United States accepted uncorroborated allegations from these militias and bounty hunters, and failed to investigate their claims about the detainees before classifying them as "enemy combatants"[10] and sending them to Guantánamo and other detention facilities.[11]

Indications that many detainees were not a serious threat to U.S. security began to surface in mid-2002. In September of that year, just eight months after the first detainees arrived at Guantánamo, high-level U.S. officials were aware of concerns within military and intelligence circles about how few of those held at Guantánamo were actually dangerous Al Qaeda or Taliban members. At the same time, a senior CIA analyst with extensive Middle East experience reportedly concluded that only approximately one-third of the population—at that time 200 of the 600 total detainees—had any connection to terrorism.[12] In 2003, an FBI counterterrorism expert told a committee of the National Security Council that there were at most 50 detainees at Guantánamo worth holding.[13]

Despite this flawed screening process, the U.S. administration branded the detainees "the worst of the worst,"[14] "bad people,"[15] and "very tough, hard core, well-trained terrorists."[16] The U.S. administration established new interrogation and detention procedures that departed sharply from international law and time-honored military practices.[17] The result was a different standard for detainee interrogation and treatment, which resulted in abuses of detainees that have been documented by government agencies[18] and nongovernmental organizations (NGOs).[19] Reported abuses include sleep deprivation, sexual humiliation, short-shackling, forced exposure to extreme temperatures, sensory bombardment with loud music and strobe lights, as well as desecration of the Qur'an.[20]

While the treatment of detainees at Guantánamo has been documented in part,[21] their fate since their release from Guantánamo is less well known. Yet reports to date are troubling. In November 2008, UC Berkeley researchers released a study, *Guantánamo and Its Aftermath: U.S. Detention and Interrogation Practices and Their Impact on Former Detainees* (hereafter "UC Berkeley Detainee Study"),[22] based on interviews with 62 released detainees in nine countries who were held in U.S. custody in Afghanistan and Guantánamo Bay. The study examined the experiences of former detainees in U.S. custody and the effect of their incarceration on their subsequent reintegration with their families and communities.[23] In addition to the UC Berkeley Detainee Study, reporters with the McClatchy Newspaper Company compiled a series of individual profiles and articles about former detainees.[24]

In the preparation of this paper, we reviewed the UC Berkeley Detainee Study, the McClatchy profiles, and a range of secondary sources, including published newspaper reports on released Guantánamo detainees,[25] relevant documents released by the Department of Defense and other U.S. agencies, and research conducted by NGOs since September 11, 2001.[26]

We compared this information to the literature on reintegration and reentry efforts in three contexts: (1) prisoners released from United States prisons; (2) former combatants participating in structured disarmament, demobilization, and reintegration (DDR) programs; and (3) prisoners of war (POWs). Each model offers a useful framework for conceptualizing an effective reintegration plan for detainees released from Guantánamo.

This policy paper has two limitations. First, we were unable to generalize from the data to the larger population of released detainees. Indeed, such generalization would require a much larger sample of former detainees and would need to employ quantitative as well as qualitative methods.[27] Second, we were unable to verify the veracity of the accounts reported in interviews with former detainees and key informants contained in the various reports. However, we found a high degree of consistency in the descriptions by former detainees of their imprisonment in Guantánamo and conditions upon returning to a country of origin or a third country, although such conditions did, in some cases, vary from country to country.

Such limitations notwithstanding, the available data enables us to identify the need for a resettlement and reintegration program and set out its key components.

Problems Faced Post-Release

Former detainees face three primary obstacles as they return to civilian life: (1) social stigma, (2) difficulty finding employment, and (3) mental and physical health problems.[28] These challenges are not unique to former Guantánamo detainees; historically, individuals returning home after periods of incarceration, exile, or war have faced similar problems. For those returning to civilian life after periods of captivity, the moment of release can be enormously difficult.[29]

Researchers have found that "lengthy exposure to the harsh, impersonal conditions" of confinement affects "an individual's ability to readjust to life outside" of that confinement, and that, "[u]ndoubtedly, ex-prisoners are changed in some way by their time in prison."[30] A 2003 study by the Center for Conflict Resolution on the lives of former combatants in postconflict zones found that 66 percent of those interviewed were unemployed, with a third suffering psychological problems.[31] In the context of child soldiers in Afghanistan, one report suggests that "[m]ost are likely suffering from psychological traumas and have been deprived of opportunities for education and civilian work."[32] Reintegration programs for former combatants seek to address the complex nature of their return through a focus on "[c]apacity building and life skills, as well as dealing with the psychological residue of the conflict."[33]

SOCIAL STIGMA

Social psychologists Jennifer Crocker, Brenda Major, and Claude Steele describe the effects of social stigma: when "social identity or membership in some social category calls into question [a person's] full humanity," then that person becomes "devalued, spoiled, or flawed in the eyes of others."[34] Vulnerable groups, particularly those involved in conflict or crime, often face stigmatization. Many former combatants may be stigmatized by the communities where they resettle due to their former combatant status, regardless of whether this community was their home before or during the conflict.[35]

Similarly, former inmates face stigmatization. A 2008 study of the attitudes of released prisoners in the United States revealed that most expected to be labeled "ex-cons" and treated as failures and pariahs.[36] The study also found that even if a former inmate was not actually devalued in the eyes of others, his or her self-perception was significantly diminished because of the fear of being stigmatized and treated differently.[37]

Many former Guantánamo detainees report feeling stigmatized as a result of their detention and have difficulty reintegrating into their communities. Detainees leave Guantánamo without having been convicted of a crime but also without official exoneration. The UC Berkeley Detainee Study found that communities often viewed former detainees as dangerous and a threat to public safety.[38] This stigmatization limited their ability to secure employment. Several former detainees said this stigma would be lifted if they had the opportunity to clear their names.[39]

The relationship between social stigma and employment is dramatic. POWs in past wars have sometimes found it difficult to secure employment, either because employers view them as too battle-scarred to hold a job or because within those societies POWs are considered a national disgrace since they were captured rather than killed honorably in battle.[40] In the context of U.S. prisons, a study found that first-time conviction in the United States significantly lowers the probability of former prisoners securing employment and generating income after release.[41]

Former Guantánamo detainees report facing similar challenges. They report that employers refuse to hire them upon learning that they have spent time in Guantánamo.[42] One former detainee reported that when he went to seek a job, he was refused employment because he was presumed to be "a dangerous person."[43] In other cases, former detainees who had worked for their home governments prior to their capture were unable to return to their former positions.

One former detainee explained that home governments "[do] not offer us any jobs because of the accusation imposed by Americans on us. The government authorities think we are terrorists."[44] Inability to obtain employment with a home government may further exacerbate social stigma by suggesting to the community that a former detainee has been determined dangerous by the authorities. In other words, if the state or the municipality will not employ a former detainee, why should a private business-owner?

Social stigmatization may also affect the mental well-being of former Guantánamo detainees. Sociologists have long understood that social integration improves mental well-being.[45] In addition to protecting an individual from psychological harm, social integration has the "ability ... to improve mental health by fulfilling a number of essential needs, both emotional and material."[46] However, many former Guantánamo detainees report receiving a mixed reception upon their return. One detainee said he felt "rejected," as if he had been classified as a dangerous person, even though he had no history of violence. Echoing similar sentiments, a former detainee said he no longer felt comfortable walking alone because of the way people in his community stared at him. Other former detainees reported trouble reestablishing social ties and that these fractured relationships led to further social exclusion. In the words of one detainee:

> Old friends, old circles, they are even afraid of greeting me because they think then they may also be taken under custody or interrogated.... Guantánamo was of short duration. It was only two years. I left Guantánamo at age 23. But it put my life in distress until the end of my life. This is a bad trade.[47]

LOSS OF ECONOMIC OPPORTUNITY

Economic stability is a crucial aspect of any successful reintegration program.[48] For example, repatriated POWs and demobilized combatants often face barriers reentering civil society due to their extended absence from the job force.[49] In the U.S. prison context, most inmates released have no savings, no immediate entitlement to unemployment benefits, and bleak job prospects. Inadequate skills, stigma of incarceration, and reentry into communities already struggling with low employment rates make economic sufficiency a major challenge to successful reintegration of former prisoners.[50]

Many former Guantánamo detainees, too, confront these issues as they try to find work after their release from detention. Only six of the 62 former detainees interviewed in the UC Berkeley Detainee Study had found permanent employment.[51] One former detainee explained: "It's impossible to get proper employment. We can only work freelance … but it is, for us, impossible to get a regular job."[52] Another respondent said he could not find any work that felt meaningful: "I am just breaking the stones on the roads for … less than two, three dollars a day."[53]

Others who did manage to find work could not always secure consistent employment or a job that was comparable to what they had held prior to their detention at Guantánamo.[54]

One former detainee, a health care professional, complained that Guantánamo had tarnished his professional reputation and made it impossible for him to resume his former career.[55] Several former detainees expressed disappointment about their job prospects. "For me and my family," one former detainee said, "the greatest need is financial because as a man, and a son, and a father, I should support my family right now."[56]

Many families have experienced financial troubles and incurred significant debt because of the absence of the primary wage earner.[57] One former detainee said that in his absence, his children were forced to borrow money to buy food.[58] Several detainees reported that their children had dropped out of school because they could not afford fees. One said his sons "quit their education because of me, and now they're going to be illiterate."[59]

Eleven Afghan respondents in the UC Berkeley Detainee Study said their families were forced to sell property, borrow money, or quit their jobs in order to finance efforts to secure their release. Five of the Afghan respondents said their relatives had paid bribes to corrupt officials or others who deceived them. "My family spent a lot of money looking for me and my shop was destroyed.... Our family borrowed a lot of money from relatives and other colleagues and there was just such a big debt and loan," one former detainee said."[60]

Paying back these debts has proved difficult.[61] Economic struggles have in many cases reshaped the lives and the futures of these men and their families. As one former detainee explained: "It's a simple life, actually. I don't have any job. There's no land now. There's no house now. And I've got such a big family, and there is no [one] responsible for my family. I don't know what to do."[62]

MENTAL AND PHYSICAL HEALTH

Harvard psychiatrist Judith Herman notes that "people who have endured horrible events suffer predictable psychological harm."[63] The harsh conditions of confinement and interrogation in Guantánamo appear to have taken a toll on the psychological health of many former detainees.

While there has been considerable focus on isolated incidents of egregious abuse,[64] relatively little attention has been paid to the *cumulative* impact of conditions on former Guantánamo detainees.

As Dr. Hernán Reyes of the International Committee of the Red Cross notes, psychological methods used in interrogations against the "'background environment' of harassment and duress" over long periods of time create a "cumulative effect" that can be a part of "a system of psychological torture."[65] According to the *Manual on Effective Investigation and Documentation of Torture and Other Cruel, Inhumane or Degrading Treatment or Punishment*, commonly known as the Istanbul Protocol:

> A method-listing approach [of torture methods] may be counter productive, as the entire clinical picture produced by torture is much more than the simple sum of lesions produced by [individual] methods on a list. Thus, solitary confinement, detention in small or overcrowded cells, exposure to extremes in temperature and deprivation of normal sensory stimulation are some torture methods whose cumulative effects over a period of time should be considered.[66]

Stuart Grassian, a psychiatrist who has studied the psychiatric effects of stringent conditions of solitary confinement, has found that such treatment can have profound effects on mental functioning and can cause long-term psychological and physical damage.[67] Grassian notes that mental disturbances can include "an agitated confusional state, characteristics of a florid delirium, [with] severe paranoid and hallucinatory features and also by intense agitation and random impulsive, often self-directed violence."[68] Additional research conducted by the National Institute of Mental Health also demonstrated "the link between captivity maltreatment and persistent psychiatric disorders."[69]

Several studies suggest that compromised psychological health impedes the reintegration of former POWs and released inmates from U.S. prisons.[70] In some cases, former POWs have experienced severe depression, substance abuse, violence, "emotional detachment from loved ones," and

"extreme suspicion of others."[71] One study showed that nine out of 10 American POWs returning from Korea were still experiencing Post Traumatic Stress Disorder (PTSD) even 30 years after their release from Korean detention.[72] Former inmates of U.S. prisons also suffer from PTSD, depression, and other mental health conditions at rates disproportionate to those of the general population.[73] Consequently, they often need targeted psychological services upon release.[74]

When asked about the most significant problems they have faced since their release from Guantánamo, many former detainees in the UC Berkeley Detainee Study said health problems were nearly of equal concern as financial troubles.[75] Many of these detainees reported facing a range of health problems, including wrist and knee pain to psychological conditions such as increased anger and agitation.[76]

Detainees attributed these problems directly to their detention and treatment in Guantánamo. One respondent received a diagnosis of PTSD from a psychiatrist.[77] Another said he now suffered from sleeplessness, insomnia, and depression—none of which he experienced before his detention at Guantánamo.[78] Some detainees also reported recurring nightmares because of their detention in Guantánamo. One respondent said: "I realized that I didn't return to this life as intact as I thought I had."[79] Another said he was still haunted by Guantánamo: "I think I'm still back there, with chains and people swearing at me."[80]

Many former detainees in the UC Berkeley Detainee Study also reported feeling detached, lonely, closed off from the world, and irritable as a result of their time in Guantánamo.[81] One former detainee said: "I lost my appetite, [feel] frustrated, distressed, and lose my temper easily. I even felt like it was better when I was in Guantánamo, because there I didn't hear anything." He finds himself unable and unwilling to interact with his family.[82] Another former detainee said that after leaving Guantánamo, he developed "a new form of aggression towards other people, which I never had before."[83]

Former Guantánamo detainees face physical health problems as well. Some in the UC Berkeley Detainee Study reported a range of physical impairments, including recurring headaches, trouble seeing clearly, fatigue or generalized deterioration, and pain in the wrists, knees, back, and ankles, all of which they attributed to their treatment in U.S. detention, including prolonged short shackling, hanging, or stress positions.[84]

These physical effects are unsurprising. Studies of former POWs document that stressors in captivity, including isolation, loss of freedom, malnourishment, disease, and torture, have been linked to short- and long-term specific health problems, including cardiovascular disease and hypertension and gastrointestinal disorders.[85] In the U.S. prison context, psychologist Craig Haney, an expert on the psychological effects of living in prison environments, has shown the consequences of long-term solitary-like confinement on prison inmates to include anxiety, panic attacks, and general deterioration of physical health.[86] Similarly, Judith Herman has found that "chronically traumatized" individuals may complain "not only of insomnia and agitation" but also of physical symptoms such as "tension headaches, gastrointestinal disturbances, and abdominal, back, or pelvic pain."[87]

The health conditions reported by former detainees suggest the interconnected nature of the problems they face post-release: Guantánamo stigma hurts their job prospects; unemployment means they are unable to provide for their families, which may contribute to vulnerability to depression and social exclusion. Former detainees may be unable to afford medical care to manage psychological or physical ailments and these ailments prevent them from finding or keeping a job. As one respondent in the UC Berkeley Detainee Study explained:

> I had a family. I had a house. I had a car. I had a job…. I was making good money. Everything was going well, and now I don't have the patience for anything…. I have problems with my physical self. I have aches in my body and my legs…. [My] life is a lot harder.[88]

Discussion

The data suggest that a significant number of former Guantánamo detainees face significant challenges as they return to their home countries or resettle in third countries. These detainees have been unable to leave behind Guantánamo completely; their experience in detention has limited their daily lives and curtailed their future opportunities. In the UC Berkeley Detainee Study, researchers reported that "most if not all" interviewees expressed "the sense that the legacy of Guantánamo remained."[89]

While further studies are necessary to understand fully the challenges facing released detainees, available data justify the need for the United States to develop a comprehensive, country-specific reintegration policy for former detainees to reduce social stigma, provide support for sustainable economic livelihoods, and make mental and physical health services available to those who desire it.

SOCIAL STIGMA

The stigmatization of former detainees can be reduced by increasing the degree of interaction other community members have with such individuals.[90] The chance for POWs to tell their stories to their communities has also been beneficial for those returning home from captivity to clarify what happened to them during their time away.[91] Historical research of POW experiences, particularly in West Germany and Japan after World War II, suggests that such public acknowledgment can be crucial for full reintegration into society.[92] Similarly, in Sierra Leone's DDR efforts, traditional cleansing and healing ceremonies and religious support helped to remove some of the barriers associated with stigma of former combatants in that country's civil war.[93]

Social reintegration efforts should draw on local resources. Local religious and community-based organizations have helped sensitize local communities to the stigma former combatants face during DDR processes in post-conflict societies.[94] Community involvement of civic and religious groups in reintegration efforts has proved effective in numerous DDR programs seeking to reintegrate ex-combatants in post-conflict zones.[95]

Reintegration programs in Nicaragua and Mozambique, for example, have successfully fostered community support through veterans associations in order to address the post-conflict needs of former soldiers seeking to readjust to civil society. The network of veterans in these countries provided support for social reintegration of former combatants, offering them counsel and advice about postwar life.[96]

The involvement of similar associations may prove effective in delivering assistance to former detainees in their communities. However, reintegration programs should not further single out released detainees from other members of their community by giving them obvious benefits that the rest of the community does not enjoy. Such practices have led to increased tensions in some instances.[97]

In addition, the opportunity for released detainees to "clear their names" through an efficient, individual process is critical. Released prisoners in the United States who are publicly certified as rehabilitated or recognized as having shown good conduct experience improved job prospects and face less hostility in society.[98] A similar process to provide official acknowledgment that released detainees pose no security threat or were wrongly detained will help them lift the Guantánamo stigma that now shadows them.

ECONOMIC REINTEGRATION

Most reentry models promote economic reintegration of participants and provide financial assistance to support short-term needs in the post-release period.[99] DDR programs include assistance with immediate needs of former combatants and can include transitional safety allowances, food, clothes, shelter, medical services, short-term education, training, employment, and tools. This phase of reinsertion can last up to one year.[100]

Released POWs in Germany also received federal funds apart from normal veterans-benefit packages because they had been away for years; these funds included lump-sum cash payments.[101] Many released Guantánamo detainees would greatly benefit from some form of immediate assistance to provide urgent financial support to their families, as well as give them an opportunity to transition back to the job force after being away for many years.

Immediate financial assistance should be coupled with a longer-term focus on securing stable employment. In U.S. prisons, this effort often begins the moment an inmate enters the prison system, and continues through various stages of his or her reentry process after release. Phased reentry, beginning with job training courses in prisons and continuing with local and charitable initiatives aimed at providing transitional jobs for former prisoners increase employment opportunities for those released.[102] DDR programs include a similar reentry process, and while implemented locally often necessitate long-term national assistance.[103]

Microfinance programs have also been part of a number of DDR efforts, including Kosovo's successful agricultural enterprise plans.[104] Similarly, POWs repatriated to West Germany received loans for starting new businesses.[105] Several of the released detainees interviewed in the UC Berkeley Detainee Study faced difficulties reestablishing their livelihoods because of increased debt. Making capital available to released detainees may prove effective in promoting economic sustainability within this population.

PROVISION OF HEALTH SERVICES

The interviews of former detainees conducted for the UC Berkeley Detainee Study point to the need for diagnosis and treatment of mental and physical conditions that detainees have faced as a result of their experiences in Guantánamo. Many former detainees will need support to reestablish trust with their families and social ties, address the impact of their absence from their families, and treat any symptoms of PTSD.

In the past, returning POWs have commonly received diagnoses of severe depression, substance abuse, violence, "emotional detachment from loved ones, [and] extreme suspicion of others."[106] Programs targeting the rehabilitation of POWs have shown that service providers must recognize the unique medical and psychological conditions that POW returnees may suffer upon reentry, particularly with regard to PTSD.

Other reentry models have focused on providing mental and physical health services in conjunction with other reintegration services, such as job training and family support. The DDR models, for instance, show that successful reintegration have traditionally included activities that have (1) strengthened an individual's coping skills for anticipated trauma and grief, (2) instilled a sense of social responsibility, and (3) promoted self-regulation and security-seeking behavior. These reintegration programs have thus emphasized the health needs of a former combatant by addressing the relationship of economic hardships and mental health problems.

Prisoners released from domestic U.S. prisons who have been exonerated from their crimes nevertheless face health problems associated with their confinement. Their experience is instructive in the context of released Guantánamo detainees. Those who have been incarcerated for crimes they committed can begin to fashion a life narrative of redemption. In contrast, those who have been wrongfully convicted cannot do so and contend with the negative psychological consequences of confinement, according to psychologist Craig Haney.[107] Many individuals released from prison after serving time on wrongful convictions need immediate assistance upon release in the form of counseling, recognition for the wrongful conviction, and validation of feelings of anger and distrust of the criminal justice system.[108] Haney notes that "the complexity of the transition from prison to home needs to be fully appreciated."[109] Provision of health services for released detainees should be available and tailored to their unique circumstances.

Policy Rationales for U.S. Support

U.S. support for reintegration of former detainees will promote U.S. foreign policy and national security interests. It will help repair the United States' tarnished image abroad resulting from Guantánamo, prevent future crimes, and initiate a paradigm shift in our counterterrorism efforts by working more collaboratively with other countries.

Further, regardless of whether the United States has a *legal* duty to assist former detainees to rebuild their lives, it has a moral duty to do so. The United States has held former detainees for years, convicted them of no crime, cut them off from their families and the world, and in many cases subjected them to cruel and inhumane treatment, if not torture. Evidence indicates that many of these men—farmers, goat-herders, laborers—were simply in the wrong place at the wrong time and should not have been detained.[110]

The United States should now help them reintegrate into their communities. And if the moral rationale for a U.S.-supported reintegration plan is compelling, the national security and foreign policy rationales for are equally strong.

REPAIRING THE U.S. REPUTATION

Many U.S. military and intelligence personnel have expressed concern about the negative impact of Guantánamo on America's image abroad. At his confirmation hearing to become Director of National Intelligence, Admiral Dennis C. Blair (Ret.) said Guantánamo was "a damaging symbol to the world."[111] Even before President Obama took office, Bush administration officials and former officials recognized that Guantánamo has diminished America's international stature.[112]

A U.S. reintegration policy for released Guantánamo detainees will begin to repair this damage and restore the nation's international reputation. Reintegration can serve an important symbolic function: a set of well-designed, U.S.-backed reintegration programs can be seen as a break from the past and a new symbol for American justice. By demonstrating the principles of humane treatment of those who have not been convicted of any wrongdoing, a reintegration program would signal the new administration's commitment to justice, human rights, transparency, and the rule of law.

PREVENTING FUTURE TERRORISM

There is a prevalent concern that detainees released from Guantánamo will become terrorists, either because of their desire to "return to the battlefield" or—if they were not involved with violence prior to detention—because their experience at Guantánamo radicalized them.[113]

The data on former Guantánamo detainees taking up arms against the United States are unclear. Statistics released by the Department of Defense have been imprecise. On January 13, 2009, Pentagon spokesman Geoff Morrell stated that 61 former detainees "appear to have returned to terrorism since their release from custody."[114] However, he added that 18 former detainees were confirmed as "returning to the fight" and 43 were suspected of having done so in a report issued late in December by the Defense Intelligence Agency.[115]

Morrell declined to give details, such as the identity of the former detainees, why and where they were released, and what actions they had taken since leaving U.S. custody.[116] The government has not provided sufficient information to enable independent verification; as a result, researchers at Seton Hall have forcefully challenged these figures as unreliable.[117]

In the past when the government has released information on Guantánamo recidivism rates, independent researchers have challenged the data.[118] Although the Department of Defense at one point publicly stated that "just short of thirty" former Guantánamo detainees have "returned" to the battlefield,[119] the Department subsequently retreated from this number.[120] In 2007, the Department released the names of detainees who had engaged in militant terrorist activities after their release from Guantánamo; the list contained only 12 names, an overall recidivism rate of just 2 percent.[121] Although some former detainees may have affiliated with terrorist organizations after their release from Guantánamo, actual recidivism rates appear to be low. And an effective reintegration program will further reduce the risk of recidivism as former detainees are supported to reestablish and maintain productive lives.

The UC Berkeley Detainee Study reported that among its sample of 62 former released detainees, many had negative feelings against the United States as a result of their experience in Guantánamo. In the UC Berkeley Detainee Study, 31 of the respondents said their opinion of the United States changed from positive to negative as a result of their experiences in U.S. custody.[122] Yet many of those who held strong negative views about the United States also affirmed their desire to address their concerns peacefully.[123] In fact, several released detainees stated they wished to assure the American people that they harbored no ill will toward them.[124]

An effective reintegration policy could mitigate the negative views that released detainees hold toward the United States and prevent released detainees from taking up arms against it. At present, Saudi Arabia is the only country with a comprehensive reintegration program for released Guantánamo detainees. This program includes religious reeducation taught by Islamic clerics; time in a halfway house where the former detainees receive religious and psychological counseling and can engage in recreational activities; help with marriage and resettlement into Saudi society; and financial support and job assistance.[125]

Until recently, Saudi Arabia claimed that no former detainees had "relapsed" into terrorism after completing its program.[126] In January 2009, however, Saudi officials announced that 11 former detainees who had been released from Guantánamo and participated in the program are now believed to have fled Saudi Arabia and joined terrorist groups abroad, although the details of all cases were not made public.[127]

An independent evaluation of the Saudi rehabilitation program is necessary to gain a full understanding of its efficacy. Reintegration programs should include safeguards to monitor former detainees after release and reduce the risk that former detainees will take up arms against the United States or its allies. Nevertheless, a comprehensive reintegration program could help reduce the risk of former detainees becoming radicalized by giving them support to address their economic troubles, isolation from social stigma, and mental and physical health problems.

BUILDING NEW STRATEGIC ALLIANCES

A U.S.-supported effort to establish reintegration programs in former detainees' home countries will also help strengthen diplomatic, military, and intelligence alliances with those countries. In this manner, reintegration programs will serve as a dramatic paradigm shift in the U.S. approach to combating terrorism worldwide—a move from unilateralism to greater multilateralism, from antagonism and strained allegiances to genuine partnerships. Such a paradigm shift is in the interest not just of the United States, but also of the released detainees' home countries, many of which face internal threats from terrorist groups.

Islamic extremist groups have used Guantánamo as a propaganda and recruitment tool to great effect. Evidence suggests that such efforts are distressingly common: researchers at West Point's Combating Terrorism Center have found scores of references by top Al Qaeda officials referencing Guantánamo, from as early as 2002 and as recently as January 2008.[128] Osama bin Laden, for instance, has referenced Guantánamo a number of times in his widely disseminated tape recordings, and has expressed outrage at "the atrocities and crimes in the prisons of Abu Ghraib and Guantánamo."[129]

Such propaganda efforts have worried government officials worldwide. Many U.S. officials fear the stain of Guantánamo has become a tool for creating more terrorists. "It is a rallying cry for terrorist recruitment and harmful to our national security, so closing it is important for our national security," Admiral Blair said in a recent statement before the Senate Select Committee on Intelligence.[130] Britain's Lord Chancellor Charles Falconer and Ernst Uhrlau, president of Germany's federal intelligence service, the Bundesnachrichtendienst (BND), have also denounced the detention facility's propaganda value for terrorist groups.[131]

Comprehensive reintegration programs would frustrate efforts of terrorists to use Guantánamo as a propaganda and recruitment tool. Localized, country-specific reintegration assistance for former detainees would drain such propaganda of much of its rhetorical power by demonstrating that the United States and the receiving country were working together to help former detainees rebuild their lives.

Further, U.S.-supported reintegration programs could also help quell religious extremist movements in the home countries of released detainees. The United States could condition reintegration aid on the establishment of local and moderate religious reeducation programs, partially modeled on the Saudi program.[132] The goal of such reeducation programs is to effectively instill the idea that "Islamic tenets [have] been perverted by Bin Laden and other terrorists," and that those terrorists are "gang leaders, not true Muslims."[133] U.S.-supported reintegration programs could thus provide a new approach in the struggle against violent extremism—an approach based on cooperation and local mores, and rooted in the core tenets of Islam.

Finally, a comprehensive resettlement and reintegration program constitutes a humanitarian response to years of confinement of former detainees in U.S. custody. However, such a program may also become part of a broader set of corrective measures to remedy the effects of detention, including providing compensation and issuing an apology or other acknowledgment of harm. The U.S. government employed this means of correction when it issued a letter of apology with reparations in 1993 to the Japanese-American survivors of domestic internment camps during World War II.[134] A reintegration program would support additional efforts to address the effects of detention on former Guantánamo detainees.

Proposal & Recommendations

We propose the establishment of comprehensive, locally-tailored resettlement and reintegration programs that would include interventions to address social stigma, job training, and medical and psychological services. Such an initiative could be implemented in a number of ways, including executive order, legislation, or an independent nonpartisan commission.

REDUCE STIGMA

Social stigma should be addressed early in the reintegration process.[135] Removing stigma will help former detainees rebuild social networks, constrain deviant behavior, and reconnect with their communities.[136] In addition to fostering stronger mental health, belonging to a solid social network also helps individuals secure employment.[137]

A reintegration program must be tailored to country-specific conditions, as the intensity of stigmatization will vary depending in part on the particular social context.[138] For example, creating opportunities for members of a community to hear from and interact with former Guantánamo detainees may occur in myriad ways—through the media, cultural ceremonies, town-hall events, or some other forum. Social stigma associated with Guantánamo can also be lessened with public education conducted by local NGOs, local governments, or religious and other respected leaders in the community.

Finally, released Guantánamo detainees would benefit from formal recognition that they do not pose a risk to society. In addition, a case-by-case process for obtaining official recognition of their innocence should also be made available. This would enable former detainees to clear their names and "rewrite" their past, and also encourage community members to work with released detainees to reintegrate them into society.[139]

ADDRESS ECONOMIC INTEGRATION

A reintegration program should support both the immediate and longer-term social and economic inclusion of former Guantánamo detainees into their communities, and can begin even during detention to ensure a smooth transition to civil society. External assistance is necessary to help the released detainees secure long-term, stable employment, which provides a steady income and a sense of structure and responsibility.

Released Guantánamo detainees would greatly benefit from an effective economic reintegration plan that targets the needs of individuals and is appropriate to the job markets in which former detainees resettle. Job-creation programs, such as small- and medium-scale enterprise development initiatives, should be a key part of the program. A microfinance model could be particularly effective for former Guantánamo detainees who struggle with debt, and for those who were previously self-employed and now need assistance to rebuild their businesses. Such support would provide released detainees an opportunity to find their own solutions to the economic challenges they face, and thus give them a sense of autonomy and ownership in their reintegration. Economic reintegration should be coordinated with local groups. Community-based organizations could initiate job transition and placement programs, and microfinance assistance for released Guantánamo detainees.

MENTAL AND PHYSICAL HEALTH

A reintegration program should support both the immediate and longer-term psychological and physical health needs of former Guantánamo detainees. It is important to ensure that released Guantánamo detainees have access to medical care appropriate to the unique circumstances of their confinement and release without conviction of a crime. Again, this aspect of reintegration assistance should be provided through local health care providers who are attuned to the cultural and social circumstances of the population and are able to tailor service delivery appropriately.

OTHER CONSIDERATIONS FOR IMPLEMENTATION

Partnership with local religious and civic organizations in designing and implementing reintegration programs should be considered so that service provision is conducted in a culturally-appropriate manner.[140]

The role that the United States should play in designing and implementing reintegration programs must be carefully considered. While the U.S. government should develop a comprehensive resettlement and reintegration policy overseen by a high-level State Department official, such as the under secretary for democracy and global affairs, it may be appropriate for the United States to support in-country implementation through local independent nongovernmental organizations. Such assistance could be administered by the U.S. Agency for International Development (USAID). Finally, there should be an effective oversight mechanism to ensure that the programs are transparent and accountable and administered efficiently.

WE PROPOSE THAT THE UNITED STATES:

» *Design a resettlement and reintegration policy to minimize the social stigma experienced by former Guantánamo detainees.* A case-by-case process should be implemented to enable former detainees to clear their names and encourage community members to assist released detainees as they reintegrate into their communities.

» *Provide released detainees with immediate short-term financial assistance and support for sustainable livelihoods.* A comprehensive reintegration program should provide immediate assistance, as well as support detainees to secure sustainable employment and income for the long-term. Preparation for re-entry into the job market should begin before release. Job training and job-creation programs, such as small- and medium-scale enterprise development initiatives, also should be a key part of the program and targeted to the local labor markets. Such support should afford released detainees an opportunity to craft their own solutions to overcome the economic challenges they face, and give them a sense of autonomy and ownership in their reintegration.

» *Support the provision of mental and physical health services for released detainees who seek such assistance.* These services should be offered in conjunction with other reintegration services, such as job training and family support. This integrated approach should address the relationship of economic hardships and mental health problems.

» *Ensure that reintegration programs are developed and implemented in partnership with local communities.* Local religious and civic organizations should be involved in the design and implementation of reintegration programs to secure the legitimacy of reintegration efforts in the home countries of former detainees. The U.S. government should develop a comprehensive resettlement and reintegration policy overseen by a high-level State Department official. However, it may be appropriate for the United States to support in-country implementation through local independent nongovernmental organizations, with appropriate monitoring and oversight.

Conclusion

The details of a U.S.-backed reintegration scheme remain to be worked out; we simply do not know enough about the released detainees as a group to make more specific recommendations. However, the known problems faced by released detainees are compelling and call for intervention. As one former detainee put it: "We can't go immediately from getting off a plane from Cuba to living in society. Everything has changed."[141]

These men, scattered across the globe, need assistance. The United States has a strategic and moral imperative to facilitate their resettlement and reintegration. A U.S.-supported reintegration plan for former Guantánamo detainees would be a wise first step.

Notes

1. Exec. Order Review and Disposition of Individuals Detained at the Guantánamo Bay Naval Base and Closure of Detention Facilities (Jan. 22, 2009) [hereinafter "Review and Disposition Order"], *available at* http://www.whitehouse. gov/the_press_office/ClosureOfGuantánamo DetentionFacilities (accessed Jan. 23, 2009). *See also* Mark Mazzetti & William Glaberson, *Obama Issues Directive to Shut Guantánamo*, N.Y. TIMES, Jan. 22, 2009; *Obama Signs Order to Close Prison at Guantánamo Bay*, BLOOMBERG, Jan. 22, 2009, *available at* http://www.bloomberg.com/apps/news?pid=20601087&sid=aA4q6b8.hGmY&refer=home (accessed Jan. 22, 2009).

2. Review and Disposition Order § 4, *supra* note 1. For those who cannot be transferred, prosecuted, or released, the order requires a lawful means of disposition of these cases. *Id.* The order further requires an immediate assessment to ensure that the men detained in Guantánamo are being held in conditions that conform "with all applicable laws … including Common Article 3 of the Geneva Conventions." *Id.* at § 6.

3. Scott Canon & David Goldstein, *With Guantánamo closing, where will the detainees go?*, McCLATCHY, Jan. 22, 2009, *available at* http://www.mcclatchydc.com/227/story/60561. html (accessed Jan. 22, 2009).

4. Press Release, U.S. Dep't of Defense, *Detainee Transfer Announced*, No. 040-09, Jan. 17, 2009, *available at* http://www. defenselink.mil/Releases/Release.aspx?ReleaseID=12449 (accessed Jan. 22, 2009). A Department of Defense list available online includes information for a total of 759 detainees detained between January 2002 and May 15, 2006. U.S. Dept. of Defense, *List of Individuals Detained by the Dep't of Defense at Guantánamo Bay, Cuba, from Jan. 2002 through May 15, 2006*, *available at* http://www.dod.mil/pubs/foi/detainees/detaineesFOIArelease15May2006.pdf (accessed Feb. 15, 2009). However, a more recent version of the list, updated by the Center for Constitutional Rights, includes information for 779 detainees. Ctr. for Constitutional Rights, *Closing Guantánamo and Restoring the Rule of Law*, *available at* http://ccrjustice.org/files/12.01.09_CCR%20Report_ Closing%20Guantánamo .pdf (accessed Feb. 15, 2009). As of January 17, 2009, 245 men remained in Guantánamo. *Detainee Transfer Announced, supra*. Of these, approximately 101 are Yemen nationals, many of whom have been cleared for release by the military status review boards but who have not returned home reportedly because the United States has not received satisfactory security assurances from the Yemeni government. Gregory D. Johnsen & Christopher Boucek, *The Dilemma of the Yemeni Detainees at Guantánamo Bay*, CTC SENTINEL, Nov. 2008, *available at* http://ctc.usma.edu/sentinel/CTCSentinel-Vol1Iss12.pdf (accessed Nov. 25, 2008). According to a Yemeni Embassy spokesman in Washington, however, there are plans for a new rehabilitation program for returned detainees which may result in increased returns. Jackie Northam, "Debate Rages Over Those Still at Guantánamo," *Morning Edition*, NAT'L PUB. RADIO, Nov. 20, 2008, *available at* http://www.npr.org/templates/story/story.php?storyId=97230217 (accessed Nov. 25, 2008); *see also* ASSOC. PRESS, *Yemenis at Gitmo stuck in diplomatic stalemate*, Jan. 11, 2008, *available at* http://www.msnbc.msn. com/id/22616052 (accessed Jan. 22, 2009).

5. *See* Human Rights Ctr. & Int'l Human Rights Law Clinic, UC Berkeley, *Guantánamo and Its Aftermath: U.S. Detention and Interrogation Practices and Their Impact on Former Detainees* (Nov. 2008) [hereinafter "UC Berkeley Detainee Study"], *available at* http://www.law.berkeley.edu/clinics/ ihrlc/pdf/Guantánamo.pdf. *See also* Amnesty International, *Life after Guantánamo: Fate of former detainees*, Dec. 10, 2007, *available at* http://www.amnesty.org/en/library/info/ AMR51/170/2007 (accessed Feb. 15, 2009).

6. Robert M. Gates, *A Balanced Strategy: Reprogramming the Pentagon for a New Age*, FOREIGN AFFAIRS, Jan./Feb. 2009.

7. Mark Denbeaux et al., *Report on Guantánamo Detainees: A Profile of 517 Detainees Through Analysis of Department of Defense Data* 25 (2006), *available at* http://law.shu.edu/ aaafinal.pdf (accessed Nov. 25, 2008). *See also* Combatant Status Review Board Letters (release dates Jan. 2005, Feb. 2005, Mar. 2005, Apr. 2005, and Final Release), available at the Seton Hall Law School library, Newark, NJ; Ken Ballen & Peter Bergen, *The Worst of the Worst?*, FOREIGN POLICY, Oct. 2008.

8. Denbeaux et al., *supra* note 7.

9. In all previous wars, the American military has followed the Geneva Conventions. Under Article 5 of the Third and Fourth Geneva Conventions, the United States has held battlefield tribunals to separate combatants and civilians. For example, in the first Gulf War, the military held 1,196 battlefield tribunals. About three-quarters of the prisoners were released through this process. Joshua Holland, *Afghanistan: The Brutal and Unnecessary War the Media Aren't Telling You About* (interview with Andy Worthington), Information Clearing House, http://www.informationclearinghouse. info/article19431.htm (accessed Nov. 16, 2008). *See also* Br. Amicus Curiae of Nat'l Institute of Military Justice in Support of Petitioners, On Writs of Certiorari to the D.C. Cir., *Boumediene v. Bush, Odah v. United States*, Nos. 05-5062 & 05-5063, Aug. 24, 2007, *available at* http://www.humanrightsfirst.org/us_law/inthecourts/gitmo_briefs/national_ institute_of_military_justice.pdf (accessed Feb. 14, 2009).

10. Under the provisions of the Secretary of the Navy Memorandum "Implementation of Combatant Status Review Tribunal Procedures for Enemy Combatant Detained at Guantánamo Bay Naval Base Cuba," an enemy combatant is defined as "an individual who was part of or supporting the Taliban or al Qaida forces, or associated forces that are engaged in hostilities against the United States or its coalition partners. This includes any person who committed a belligerent act or has directly supported hostilities in aid of enemy armed forces." Secretary of the Navy Gordon England, Memorandum, July 29, 2004, *available at* http://www.defenselink.mil/news/Jul2004/d20040730comb.pdf (accessed March 6, 2009).

11. Ballen & Bergen, *supra* note 7.

12. JANE MAYER, THE DARK SIDE: THE INSIDE STORY OF HOW THE WAR ON TERROR TURNED INTO A WAR ON AMERICAN IDEALS 183 (2008).

13. *Id.* at 187.

14. Katharine Q. Seelye, *Some Guantánamo Prisoners Will Be Freed, Rumsfeld Says*, N.Y. TIMES, Oct. 23, 2002, *available at* http://query.nytimes.com/gst/fullpage.html?res=9800E FD7143CF930A15753C1A9649C8B63 (accessed Feb. 24, 2009).

15. Press Conference of President Bush & British Prime Minister Tony Blair, July 17, 2003, *available at* http://www.npr.org/templates/story/story.php?storyId=1340673 (accessed Feb. 28, 2009).

16. Secretary of Defense Donald Rumsfeld, Media Stakeout at NBC, Jan. 20, 2002, *available at* http://www.defenselink.mil/transcripts/transcript.aspx?transcriptid=2243 (accessed Nov. 30, 2008).

17. *See generally* PHILLIPE SANDS, TORTURE TEAM (2008); MAYER, *supra* note 12.

18. *See, e.g.*, Bob Woodward, *Detainee Tortured, Says U.S. Official*, WASH. POST, January 14, 2009 (interview with Susan J. Crawford, convening authority of military commissions); U.S. Dept. of Justice, Office of the Inspector General, *A Review of the FBI's Involvement in and Observations of Detainee Interrogations in Guantánamo Bay, Afghanistan, and Iraq* 170, May 20, 2008, *available at* http://www.aclu.org/safefree/torture/35402lgl20080520.html (accessed Feb. 23, 2009); Adm. Albert T. Church III, *Review of Department of Defense Detention Operations and Detainee Interrogation Techniques: Executive Summary* 168, March 11, 2005, *available at* http://humanrights.ucdavis.edu/resources/library/documents-and-reports/ChurchReport.pdf; U.S. Dept. of Defense, *Army Regulation 15-6: Final Report, Investigation into FBI Allegations of Detainee Abuse at Guantánamo Bay, Cuba Detention Facility* 12, April 1, 2005, amended June 9, 2005, *available at* http://www.defenselink.mil/news/Jul2005/d20050714report.pdf.

19. *See* Human Rights Watch, *Locked Up Alone: Detention Conditions and Mental Health at Guantánamo*, June 10, 2008, *available at* http://www.hrw.org/en/node/62183/section/1 (accessed Feb. 23, 2009). *See also* Ctr. for Constitutional Rights, *Foreign Interrogators in Guantánamo Bay, available at* http://ccrjustice.org/learn-more/faqs/foreign-interrogators-Guantánamo-bay (accessed Feb. 23, 2009).

20. *See, e.g.*, William Glaberson, *Red Cross Monitors Barred from Guantánamo*, N.Y. TIMES, November 16, 2007, *available at* http://www.nytimes.com/2007/11/16/washington/16gitmo.html (accessed Feb. 23, 2009); JAMES YEE, FOR GOD AND COUNTRY: FAITH AND PATRIOTISM UNDER FIRE (2005); Human Rights Watch, *Locked Up Alone, supra* note 19.

21. MAYER, *supra* note 12; SANDS, *supra* note 17; MAHVISH KHAN, MY GUANTÁNAMO DIARY (2008); MURAT KURNAZ, FIVE YEARS OF MY LIFE: AN INNOCENT MAN IN GUANTÁNAMO (2008); CLIVE STAFFORD SMITH, EIGHT O'CLOCK FERRY TO THE WINDWARD SIDE: SEEKING JUSTICE IN GUANTÁNAMO BAY (2007); ANDY WORTHINGTON, THE GUANTÁNAMO FILES (2007); MOAZZAM BEGG, ENEMY COMBATANT (2007); FREDERICK A.O. SCHWARZ JR. & AZIZ Z. HUQ, UNCHECKED AND UNBALANCED (2007).

22. UC Berkeley Detainee Study, *supra* note 5.

23. This paper expands the findings of the UC Berkeley Detainee Study on return and reintegration. Researchers collected these data through a semistructured questionnaire in interviews with 62 former detainees in 9 countries. For a full description of the data collection and analysis methodology, see UC Berkeley Detainee Study, *supra* note 5 at 13–15.

24. Beginning in March 2007, reporters from the McClatchy Newspaper Company spent eight months traveling to 11 countries, interviewing 66 former Guantánamo detainees about their experiences in detention systems at Guantánamo and in Afghanistan. *See* McClatchy Detainee Profiles, http://detainees.mcclatchydc.com.

25. As part of the UC Berkeley Detainee Study, researchers compiled a media database that included newspaper articles from January 2002–December 2006. *See* UC Berkeley Detainee Study, *supra* note 5, at 14 (describing the details of this media database).

26. *See, e.g.*, *Closing Guantánamo and Restoring the Rule of Law, supra* note 4; ACLU, *Enduring Abuse: Torture and Cruel Treatment by the United States at Home and Abroad*, Apr. 27, 2006, *available at* http://www.aclu.org/safefree/torture/torture_report.pdf (accessed Feb. 23, 2009); Amnesty Int'l, *Cruel and Inhuman: Conditions of isolation for detainees at Guantánamo Bay*, Apr. 5, 2007, *available at* http://www.amnesty.org/en/library/info/AMR51/051/2007 (accessed Feb. 23, 2009); Human Rights Watch, *By the Numbers: Findings of the Detainee Abuse and Accountability Project*, Apr. 25, 2006, *available at* http://www.hrw.org/en/reports/2006/04/25/numbers-0 (accessed Feb. 23, 2009); Human Rights First & Physicians for Human Rights, *Leave No Marks: Enhanced Interrogation Techniques and the Risk of Criminality*, Aug. 2007, *available at* http://www.humanrightsfirst.info/pdf/07801-etn-leave-no-marks.pdf (accessed Feb. 23, 2009).

27. Collection of such quantitative data regarding released detainees could be accomplished through the work of an independent commission, as recommended in the UC Berkeley

Detainee Study. *See* UC Berkeley Detainee Study, *supra* note 5, at 5–6.

28. Severe persecution and abuse of former detainees by home governments after release has been documented. *See* Human Rights Watch, *The "Stamp of Guantánamo:" The Story of Seven Men Betrayed by Russia's Diplomatic Assurances to the United States*, Mar. 2007, *available at* http://www.hrw.org/en/node/10989/section/1 (accessed Feb. 23, 2009); Human Rights Watch, *Ill-Fated Homecomings: A Tunisian Case Study of Guantánamo*, Sept. 2007, *available at* http://www.hrw.org/en/reports/2007/09/04/ill-fated-homecomings (accessed Feb. 23, 2009). However, the available data suggest that the number of former detainees who have faced such mistreatment is relatively low. According to the Department of Defense, most Guantánamo detainees who have been transferred into detention in their home countries were quickly released. *See* Declaration of Sandra L. Hodgkinson, Deputy Assistant Secretary of Defense for Detainee Affairs, U.S. Dep't of Defense § 5, cited in UC Berkeley Detainee Study, *supra* note 5, at 62. This finding is consistent with the UC Berkeley Detainee Study, which found that 45 of 62 former detainees were released from government custody within 72 hours of arrival. *Id.*

29. Christy A. Visher & Jeremy Travis, *Transitions from Prison to Community: Understanding Individual Pathways*, 29 ANN. REV. SOCIOLOGY 89, 96 (2003). *See also* Jeremy Travis, Amy L. Solomon, Michelle Waul, *From prison to home: the dimensions and consequences of prisoner reentry* (2001), http://www.urban.org/publications/410098.html (accessed Feb. 15, 2009).

30. Visher & Travis, *supra* note 29, at 96.

31. Gwinyayi Dzinesa, *Postconflict Disarmament, Demobilization, and Reintegration of Former Combatants in Southern Africa*, 8 INT'L STUDIES PERSPECTIVES 73–89 (2007).

32. Mark Sedra, *New Beginning or Return to Arms? The Disarmament, Demobilization & Reintegration Process in Afghanistan* (working paper discussed at the ZEF-LSE workshop "State Reconstruction and International Engagement in Afghanistan"), *available at* http://www.ag-afghanistan.de/arg/arp/sedra.pdf (accessed Feb. 23, 2009).

33. KOFF Centre for Peacebuilding, Nov. 2007 Newsletter 4–6, http://www.swisspeace.ch/typo3/fileadmin/user_upload/pdf/KOFF/Newsletter/2007/62_e.pdf (accessed Feb. 23, 2009).

34. Jennifer Crocker & Dianne Quinn, *Psychological Consequences of Devalued Identity*, in SELF & SOCIAL IDENTITY 124 (Marilynn Brewer & Miles Hewstone eds. 2004).

35. Sanam Naraghi Anderlini & Camille Pampell Conaway, "Disarmament, Demobilisation and Reintegration," *Inclusive Security, Sustainable Peace: A Toolkit for Advocacy and Action* (Nov. 2004), http://www.huntalternatives.org/download/31_disarmament.pdf (accessed Sept. 16, 2008).

36. Terri A. Winnick & Mark Bodkin, *Anticipated stigma and stigma management among those to be labeled "ex-con,"* 29 DEVIANT BEHAVIOR 295, 321 (2008).

37. *Id.*

38. UC Berkeley Detainee Study, *supra* note 5, at 63. A statement accompanying a recent Amnesty International report, "Life after Guantánamo," which contains testimonies from former detainees and their relatives, stated that "once a person is picked up and labeled an 'enemy combatant' by the United States, his life becomes one of constant torment and stigma." Abid Aslam, *What Happens After They Leave Guantánamo?*, Feb. 6, 2006, *available at* http://www.commondreams.org/headlines06/0206-02.htm (accessed Feb. 15, 2009).

39. UC Berkeley Detainee Study, *supra* note 5, at 70–71.

40. *See, e.g.,* ULRICH STRAUS, THE ANGUISH OF SURRENDER: JAPANESE POWs OF WORLD WAR II 3 (2005); Hiroo Sekita, "U.S.–Japan Dialogue on POWs: In Response to POW Story by Father Robert W. Phillips," http://www.us-japandialogueonpows.org/Phillips.htm (accessed Feb. 23, 2009) (noting that "Japanese soldiers were indoctrinated with the idea that it was the utmost shame for an Emperor's soldier to become a POW at the battlefield").

41. Joel Waldfogel, *The Effect of Criminal Conviction on Income and the Trust "Reposed in the Workmen,"* 29 J. HUMAN RESOURCES 62, 63 (1994). The study linked the difficulty of finding work directly to the stigmatizing effect of conviction, and not just to job displacement or the fact that released prisoners have been out of the workforce.

42. UC Berkeley Detainee Study, *supra* note 5, at 67.

43. UC Berkeley Detainee Study Interview Transcripts (unpublished).

44. *Id.*

45. Christine H. Lindquist, *Social Integration and Mental Well-Being Among Jail Inmates*, 15(3) SOCIOLOGICAL FORUM 431, 432 (2000).

46. *Id.*

47. UC Berkeley Detainee Study Interview Transcripts (unpublished).

48. *See* U.N. Disarmament, Demobilization and Reintegration Resource Centre (UNDDR), "Social and Economic Reintegration," http://www.unddr.org/iddrs/04/30.php (accessed Feb. 20, 2009); *see also* Visher & Travis, *supra* note 29, at 96–97.

49. *See, e.g.,* Bruce Bower, *Emotional Trauma Haunts Korean POWs*, 139(5) SCIENCE NEWS 68 (1991).

50. Joan Petersilia, *When Prisoners Return to the Community: Political, Economic, and Social Consequences*, SENTENC-

ING & CORRECTIONS: ISSUES FOR THE 21ST CENTURY 3 (Nov. 2000), *available at* http://www.ncjrs.gov/pdffiles1/nij/184253.pdf (accessed Sept. 20, 2008). *See also* Anderlini & Conaway, *supra* note 35.

51. UC Berkeley Detainee Study, *supra* note 5, at 67.

52. UC Berkeley Detainee Study Interview Transcripts (unpublished).

53. *Id.*

54. UC Berkeley Detainee Study, *supra* note 5, at 67.

55. *Id.*

56. *Id.* at 66.

57. HELEN CODD, IN THE SHADOW OF PRISON: FAMILIES, IMPRISONMENT AND CRIMINAL JUSTICE 52–56 (2008).

58. UC Berkeley Detainee Study Interview Transcripts (unpublished).

59. UC Berkeley Detainee Study, *supra* note 5, at 65.

60. UC Berkeley Detainee Study Interview Transcripts (unpublished).

61. UC Berkeley Detainee Study, *supra* note 5, at 66–67.

62. UC Berkeley Detainee Study Interview Transcripts (unpublished).

63. JUDITH HERMAN, TRAUMA AND RECOVERY: THE AFTERMATH OF VIOLENCE—FROM DOMESTIC ABUSE TO POLITICAL TERROR 3 (1997).

64. *See A Review of the FBI's Involvement in and Observations of Detainee Interrogations, supra* note 18; Adm. Church, *supra* note 18; *Army Regulation 15-6, supra* note 18; *Locked Up Alone, supra* note 19; *Foreign Interrogators in Guantánamo Bay, supra* note 19; MAYER, *supra* note 12; KHAN, *supra* note 21; WORTHINGTON, *supra* note 21; SANDS, *supra* note 17; KURNAZ, *supra* note 21.

65. Hernán Reyes, *The Worst Scars Are in the Mind: Psychological Torture,* 867 INT'L REV. RED CROSS 89 (Sept. 2007).

66. *Istanbul Protocol: Manual on the Effective Investigation and Documentation of Torture and Other Cruel, Inhuman or Degrading Treatment or Punishment* 37, *available at* http://physiciansforhumanrights.org/library/documents/reports/istanbul-protocol.pdf (accessed Feb. 25, 2009).

67. *See* Stuart Grassian, *Psychiatric Effects of Solitary Confinement,* 22 WASH. U. J. L. & POL'Y 325 (2006).

68. *Id. See also* UC Berkeley Detainee Study, *supra* note 5, at 49, 101.

69. ELLEN T. GERRITY ET AL., THE MENTAL HEALTH CONSEQUENCES OF TORTURE 144 (2001).

70. Society for Science & the Public, *Healthier Adjustment for Vietnam POWs,* 112(12) SCIENCE NEWS 182 (1977). *See also* Bower, *supra* note 49.

71. *See* Bower, *supra* note 49; Hamilton I. McCubin et al., *The Returned Prisoner of War: Factors in Family Reintegration,* 37(3) J. MARRIAGE & FAMILY 471 (1975); D. Stephen Nice et al., *The Families of U.S. Navy Prisoners of War from Vietnam Five Years after Reunion,* 43(2) J. MARRIAGE & FAMILY 431 (1981).

72. Bower, *supra* note 49.

73. Jeremy Travis et al., *Urban Institute Justice Policy Center, From Prison to Home: The Dimensions and Consequences of Prisoner Reentry* 27–30 (2001), http://www.urban.org/url.cfm?ID=410098 (accessed Feb. 24, 2009).

74. Theodore M. Hammett et al., *Health-Related Issues in Prisoner Reentry,* 47 CRIME & DELINQUENCY 390, 390–91 (2001). *See also* Craig Haney, *The Psychological Impact of Incarceration: Implications for Post-Prison Adjustment,* in FROM PRISON TO HOME: THE EFFECT OF INCARCERATION AND REENTRY ON CHILDREN, FAMILIES, AND COMMUNITIES, U.S. Dept. of Health & Human Svcs., *available at* http://aspe.hhs.gov/hsp/prison2home02/haney.pdf (accessed Feb. 24, 2009). A study of former combatants participating in a DDR program in Nicaragua assessed the psychological conditions of 82 former combatants who had been injured in battle. Nearly five years after they had sustained injuries, these individuals still suffered from PTSD and other forms of mental and social dysfunction that affected their long-term psychosocial outcomes. *See* Brian Engdahl et al., *Former Combatants,* in TRAUMA INTERVENTIONS IN WAR AND PEACE: PREVENTION, PRACTICE, & POLICY 277 (Bonnie L. Green et al. eds. 2003).

75. The former detainees interviewed in the UC Berkeley Detainee Study self-reported their physical and emotional problems. Researchers did not conduct medical and psychological evaluations of the respondents.

76. UC Berkeley Detainee Study, *supra* note 5, at 68.

77. *See* HERMAN, *supra* note 63 (providing a detailed analysis of PTSD in victims of chronic abuse).

78. UC Berkeley Detainee Study Interview Transcripts (unpublished).

79. *Id.*

80. UC Berkeley Detainee Study, *supra* note 5, at 68.

81. UC Berkeley Detainee Study Interview Transcripts (unpublished).

82. *Id.*

83. *Id.*

84. *Id.*

85. P.R.J. Falger, *Current posttraumatic stress disorder and cardiovascular disease risk factors in Dutch Resistance veterans*

from World War II, 57 PSYCHOTHERAPY & PSYCHOSOMAT-ICS 164, 164–71 (1992). *See also* Sarah E. Ullman & Judith M. Siegel, *Traumatic events and physical health in a community sample*, 9(4) J. TRAUMATIC STRESS 703 (1996); Brett T. Litz et al., *Physical complaints in combat related post-traumatic stress disorder: A preliminary report*, 5(1) J. TRAUMATIC STRESS 131 (1992).

86. Haney distinguishes between solitary confinement and "solitary-like" confinement: the latter he describes as confinement where prisoners are kept under conditions of "unprecedented levels of social deprivation for unprecedented lengths of time." Haney, *supra* note 74, at 14.

87. HERMAN, *supra* note 63, at 86.

88. UC Berkeley Detainee Study Interview Transcripts (unpublished).

89. UC Berkeley Detainee Study, *supra* note 5, at 73.

90. Robert E. Kleck, *Physical stigma and nonverbal cues emitted in face-to-face interaction*, 21(1) HUMAN RELATIONS 119 (1968).

91. *See* STRAUS, *supra* note 40.

92. *Id. See also* FRANK BIESS, HOMECOMINGS: RETURNING POWS AND THE LEGACIES OF DEFEAT IN POSTWAR GERMANY 184 (2006) (explaining that the homecoming ceremonies for POWs were designed to remove the stigma of being captured rather than dying in battle).

93. John Williamson, *The disarmament, demobilization and reintegration of child soldiers: social and psychological transformation in Sierra Leone*, 4(3) INTERVENTION 193, 185–205 (2006), *available at* http://www.usaid.gov/our_work/humanitarian_assistance/the_funds/pubs/sl_reintegration3_07.pdf (accessed Feb. 25, 2009). *See generally* Clifford Bernath & Sayre Nyce, Refugees International, *UNAMSIL—A Peacekeeping Success: Lessons Learned* (2002), *available at* http://www.reliefweb.int/rw/RWFiles2002.nsf/FilesByRWDocUNIDFileName/ACOS-64DBFM-ri-sil-18oct.pdf/$File/ri-sil-18oct.pdf (accessed Feb. 24, 2009).

94. UNDDR, *Post-Post-Conflict Stabilization, Peace-Building and Recovery Frameworks*, http://www.unddr.org/iddrs/02/20.php (accessed Nov. 26, 2008) (noting that "local leaders and community groups such as women's groups or religious societies can be important allies in the information-sharing and sensitization processes needed to support and encourage DDR, and in helping to persuade people in armed groups and forces to join the DDR process and local communities to accept the return of former combatants into a community").

95. U.S. Agency for Int'l Dev. (USAID), *OTI Special Focus Areas: Reintegrating Ex-Combatants*, http://www.usaid.gov/our_work/crosscutting_programs/transition_initiatives/focus/excombat.html (accessed Feb. 24, 2009) (discussing the relevance of community-based programs).

96. Creative Assoc. Int'l, Inc. & USAID Bur. for Humanitarian Response, Office of Transition Initiatives, *Other country experiences in demobilization and reintegration of ex-combatants: workshop, proceedings, and case study findings* (April 1995) (showing effectiveness of USAID programs that link veterans and non-veterans). *See also* Massimo Fusato, *Disarmament, Demobilization, and Reintegration of Ex-Combatants* (July 2003), *available at* http://peacestudies.conflictresearch.org/essay/demobilization/?nid=1376 (accessed Feb. 25, 2009) (noting that place of relocation along with information on economic institutions and social networks such as veterans associations, religious groups, farmers' associations should be provided in post-discharge situations in the DDR context).

97. In the DDR context, for example, targeted programs can be misconstrued to be partial and preferential treatment to ex-combatants as opposed to other displaced communities, resulting in further civic tension and isolation from their community. *See* DENISE SPENCER, DEMOBILIZATION AND REINTEGRATION IN CENTRAL AMERICA (1997).

98. April Frazier & Margaret Love, *Certificates of Rehabilitation and Other Forms of Relief from the Collateral Consequences of Conviction: A Survey of State Laws*, ABA Commission on Effective Criminal Sanctions (Sept. 19, 2006), *available at* http://www.saferfoundation.org/docs/AllStates-Briefing-Sheet91906_2_.pdf (accessed Feb. 25, 2009).

99. JOAO GOMES PORTO ET AL., SOLDIERS TO CITIZENS: DEMILITARISATION OF CONFLICT AND SOCIETY 19–20 (2007).

100. UNDDR, *supra* note 94.

101. ROBERT MOELLER, WAR STORIES: THE SEARCH FOR A USABLE PAST IN THE FEDERAL REPUBLIC OF GERMANY 45 (2001).

102. Dan Bloom et al., *Transitional Jobs for Ex-Prisoners: Early Impacts from a Random Assignment Evaluation of the Center for Employment Opportunities (CEO) Prisoner Reentry Program* (Nov. 2007), *available at* http://www.mdrc.org/publications/468/overview.html (accessed Feb. 25, 2009).

103. UNDDR, *supra* note 94.

104. Anderlini & Conaway, *supra* note 35.

105. MOELLER, *supra* note 101.

106. *See* Bower, *supra* note 49; McCubin et al., *supra* note 71; Nice et al., *supra* note 71, at 431–37.

107. *See* Interview with Craig Haney, "Burden of Innocence," *Frontline, available at* http://www.pbs.org/wgbh/pages/frontline/shows/burden/interviews/haney.html (accessed Feb. 25, 2009).

108. Illinois Criminal Justice Info. Auth., *The Needs of the Wrongfully Convicted: A Report on a Panel Discussion* (2002), *available at* http://www.law.northwestern.edu/wrongfulconvictions/issues/afterexoneration/ilpanelrpt.html (accessed

Feb. 25, 2009). There is also a growing recognition that there are public health benefits, as well as improvements in the success of individuals in reintegrating with their communities when they receive proper healthcare beyond the prison gates. As a result, researchers have proposed and studied a number of best practices and model programs, and recommended that correctional facilities improve programs for discharge planning, community linkages, and continuity of care for all released inmates. Hammett et al., *supra*, note 74 at 390.

109. Haney, *supra* note 74. *See also* Thomas A. Campbell, *Psychological assessment, diagnosis, and treatment of torture survivors: A review*, 27(5) CLINICAL PSYCH. REV. 628–41 (2007).

110. *See* Haney, *supra* note 107; Illinois Criminal Justice Info. Auth., *supra* note 108.

111. William Glaberson & Mark Mazzetti , *Obama Issues Directive to Shut Guantánamo*, N.Y. TIMES, January 22, 2009.

112. Admiral Mike Mullen, Chairman of the Joint Chiefs of Staff, said in January 2008 that he favored closing Guantánamo in order to repair the U.S. image abroad. As-soc. PRESS, *Chief of U.S. Military Says Close Guantánamo to Salvage U.S. Image*, January 13, 2008, *available at* http://www.foxnews.com/story/0,2933,322442,00.html (accessed February 25, 2009). Ken Robinson, who served for 20 years in the CIA and NSA, said, "Our place in the world has been eroded" by Guantánamo, and "[w]e have lost the moral high ground." Agence France-Presse, *Harsh interrogation methods stain US image, endanger soldiers: experts*, June 18, 2008, *available at* http://rawstory.com/news/afp/Harsh_interrogation_methods_stain_U_06182008.html (accessed Feb. 25, 2009).

113. *See, e.g.*, Tom Lasseter, *How Gitmo became a terror training ground*, MIAMI HERALD, June 17, 2008.

114. David Morgan, *Pentagon: 61 ex-Guantánamo inmates return to terrorism*, REUTERS, January 13, 2009, *available at* http://www.reuters.com/article/topNews/idUSTRE50C5JX20090113?sp=true (accessed Jan. 15, 2009).

115. *Id.*

116. *Id.*

117. Seton Hall researchers are especially critical of these figures because they do not include "names, dates, places nor any conduct by released detainees." Mark Denbeaux et al., *Released Guantánamo Detainees and the Department of Defense: Propoganda by the Numbers?* (Jan. 15, 2009), http://law.shu.edu/center_policyresearch/reports/propoganda_numbers_11509.pdf (accessed Jan. 22, 2009).

118. *Id.*

119. U.S. Dept. of Defense, *Former Guantánamo detainees who have returned to the fight*, July 2007, http://www.nefafoundation.org/miscellaneous/FeaturedDocs/DOD_fmrGitmo.pdf. (accessed Feb. 25, 2009).

120. Seton Hall Ctr. for Pol'y & Research, *Justice Scalia, the Department of Defense, and the Perpetuation of an Urban Legend: The Truth about Recidivism of Released Guantánamo Detainees* 6 (August 4, 2008), *available at* http://law.shu.edu/center_policyresearch/reports/urban_legend_final_61608.pdf (accessed Feb. 25, 2009).

121. Of these 12 former detainees, the Pentagon cites only six instances in which a released detainee fought against the United States. Ballen & Bergen, *supra* note 7. By comparison, the recidivism rate in the United States is about 67%, according to a June 2006 U.S. prison study by the bipartisan Commission on Safety and Abuse in America's Prisons. John J. Gibbons & Nicholas de B. Katzenbach, *Commission of Safety and Abuse in America's Prisons, Confronting Confinement: A Report of the Commission on Safety and Abuse in America's Prisons* (June 2006), http://www.prisoncommission.org/pdfs/Confronting_Confinement.pdf (accessed Feb. 25, 2009).

122. UC Berkeley Detainee Study, *supra* note 5, at 71.

123. *Id.*

124. *Id.*

125. *See* Christopher Boucek, *Extremist Reeducation and Rehabilitation in Saudi Arabia*, 5(16) TERRORISM MONITOR 2 (2007); Caryle Murphy, *Saudis use cash and counseling to fight terrorism*, CHRISTIAN SCIENCE MONITOR, August 20, 2008; Shiraz Maher, *A Betty Ford Clinic for Jihadis*, SUNDAY TIMES (London), July 6, 2008; Katherine Zoepf, *Deprogramming Jihadists*, N.Y. TIMES MAGAZINE, November 7, 2008.

126. Farah Stockman, *Nationality plays role in detainee release*, BOSTON GLOBE, Nov. 22, 2007.

127. Robert F. Worth, *Freed by the U.S., Saudi Becomes a Qaeda Chief*, N.Y. TIMES, Jan. 22, 2009. *See also* Robert F. Worth, *Saudis issue list of 85 Detainees*, N.Y. TIMES, February 3, 2009.

128. Sarah E. Mendelson, Center for Strategic & Int'l Studies, *Closing Guantánamo: From Bumper Sticker to Blueprint* 5, Sept. 2008, http://www.csis.org/media/csis/pubs/080905_mendelson_Guantánamo_web.pdf (accessed Feb. 25, 2009).

129. BBC, "Text: bin-Laden tape," Jan. 19, 2006, http://news.bbc.co.uk/2/hi/middle_east/4628932.stm. *See also* MSNBC, "Osama bin Laden tape transcript," May 23, 2006, http://www.msnbc.msn.com/id/12939961 (accessed Feb. 26, 2009).

130. Dennis Blair, Statement before U.S. Senate Select Comm. on Intelligence, Jan. 22, 2009, *available at* http://www.nytimes.com/2009/01/22/us/politics/23blair-text.html?ref=politics (accessed Feb. 26, 2009). Similarly, then-Senator Joseph Biden called Guantánamo "the greatest propaganda tool that exists for recruiting of terrorists around the world." David Usborne, *Terrorists "using Guantánamo as a recruitment aid*," INDEPENDENT, June 6, 2005.

131. *See* AGENCE FRANCE-PRESSE, *British justice minister says Guantánamo is "recruiting agent" for terrorism*, June 14, 2006; DER SPIEGEL, *Guantánamo Sends the Wrong Signal to the Muslim World*, April 4, 2007, http://www.spiegel.de/international/germany/0,1518,475676,00.html (accessed Feb. 16, 2009).

132. Jeffrey Fleishman, *Saudi Arabia tries to rehab radical minds*, L.A. TIMES, Dec. 21, 2007.

133. *Id.*

134. President Bill Clinton, Letter of apology to Japanese survivors of WWII internment camps, *available at* http://www.landmarkcases.org/korematsu/leterofapology.html (accessed Feb. 26, 2009).

135. Michelle R. Hebl & Robert. E. Kleck, *Virtually Interactive: A New Paradigm for the Analysis of Stigma Virtually Interactive: A New Paradigm for the Analysis of Stigma*, 13(2) PSYCH. INQUIRY 128, 128–132 (2002).

136. Elizabeth Craft & Sheldon Stryker, *Deviance, Selves and Others Revisited*, 14 YOUTH & SOCIETY 159 (1982).

137. MARK GRANOVETTER, GETTING A JOB: A STUDY OF CONTACTS & CAREERS 17–18 (1995).

138. *Id.* at 105.

139. Carrie A. Pettus & Margaret Severson, *Paving The Way For Effective Reentry Practice: The Critical Role And Function Of The Boundary Spanner*, 86(2) PRISON J. 206, 210–211 (2006).

140. One such partnership was South Africa's post-Apartheid Truth and Reconciliation Commission (TRC), chaired by Archbishop Desmond Tutu, who "officiated at the [TRC] hearings as if he were conducting a sacred service—opening with prayer, leading hymns and lighting holy candles in memory of those who had sacrificed themselves." Lyn S. Graybill, *Pardon, punishment, and amnesia: three African post-conflict methods*, 25(6) THIRD WORLD Q. 1117, 1118 (2004). *See also* Noel Muchenga Chicuecue, *Reconciliation: The Role of Truth Commissions and Alternative Ways of Healing*, 7(4) DEVELOPMENT IN PRACTICE 483 (1997).

141. Fleishman, *supra* note 132.

Authors & Acknowledgments

AUTHORS Nandini Iyer
Krista Kshatriya
Jonas Lerman
Laura Weitzman

The authors are J.D. candidates at the University of California, Berkeley, School of Law (2010). They conducted this work as interns in the school's International Human Rights Law Clinic.

EDITORS Laurel E. Fletcher
Director, International Human Rights Law Clinic
Clinical Professor of Law
University of California, Berkeley, School of Law

Eric Stover
Faculty Director, Human Rights Center
Adjunct Professor of Law and Public Health
University of California, Berkeley

DESIGN Jonas Lerman Studio, San Francisco, CA

COVER PHOTO Andreas Lunde, "The Taurus Express" (2008)

ACKNOWLEDGMENTS The authors thank Carolyn Patty Blum at the Center for Constitutional Rights for reviewing drafts of this paper and offering perceptive suggestions; Stephen P. Smith for technical training; Roxanna Altholz and Jamie O'Connell at the International Human Rights Law Clinic for their guidance and support; and Camille Crittenden with the Human Rights Center for editing the paper. The Berkeley Law library staff provided invaluable research support. The authors also thank Dean Christopher Edley, Jr., for his commitment to clinical education and support of the project.

The authors are grateful to the individual donors to the International Human Rights Law Clinic and Human Rights Center without whom this work would not be possible. Travel support for this project was provided by the Rosalinde and Arthur Gilbert Foundation.

CPSIA information can be obtained at www.ICGtesting.com
Printed in the USA
266815BV00003BA/11/P